D0018341

depression & other magic tricks

sabrina benaim

DEPRESSION & OTHER MAGIC TRICKS

POEMS BY

Sabrina Benaim

—

Published by Button Poetry / Exploding Pinecone Press
Minneapolis, MN 55403 | http://www.buttonpoetry.com

—

Manufactured in the United States of America

Cover Design: Nikki Clark

ISBN 978-1-943735-20-4

first date

hello. when i say hello, i mean thank you. when i say thank you, i mean i adore you. when i say i adore you, i mean i will check your horoscope. i mean when you leave the balloons that you carry in your laughter behind on my ceiling, well, i like them better than flowers. my body is a garden rooted in gratitude. thank you is the biggest poem i've got inside of me. oh, me? i am a campfire cold hearts like to sit around and roast their marshmallows in. when i say campfire, i mean tiny furnace, little light lady. i mean i am not the path of least resistance. but i swear, i was struck by lightning. bang! boom! wow!   this one time at Coachella when Jay-Z brought out Beyoncé - i mean, i am flawless... procrastinator. my heart is a messy bedroom i always distract myself from cleaning. i digress...when i say Beyoncé came out, i mean fireworks went off and i cried. when i say i cried, i mean i taught the clouds how to cry for me, dig?   i wouldn't say i'm sensitive, i would say i'm highly susceptible to feeling a lot, and "sometimes there just ain't enough rocks." Forrest Gump. when i say my feelings are a box of chocolates, i mean i like to eat them. i also like to get high enough to look myself in the third eye. when i say i like to get high, i mean, sometimes, after i shower i thank the towel. snap, crackle, or pop? me? pop. i mean i've got this violent tendency to see a bubble and want to pop it. which is to say: i have held love, but i popped it and locked it, then dropped it and lost it. i didn't mind. love made me feel like i knew the answer, but when i raised my hand, i was the only one in the room. what i mean is, have you ever felt the ache of swallowing starlight? that cinnamon heartburn? what i mean is, his name is a plate set at the table of my tongue because i learned love like wait for it.   if i called the last person you said i love you to could they tell me they felt it? can you feel this? i'm allergic to li-ars, they cause my tongue to swell and sharpen; bullet flesh tongue. what i mean is my kiss tastes like a shotgun to the lips. you'll like it. it'll make you feel brave.   my first crush was on Benny 'The Jet' Rodriguez. that boy ran so fast, he could fly by foot. if i were an animal, i would be a hummingbird. when i say hummingbird, i mean sometimes my hands forget how to hold, become two teacups in an earthquake. i am a rattle of splintered bones. when i say my body, i mean blunt guts and then some. my instincts are miraculous. i spent an entire year sleeping on a bed of swords and was not cut once. what i mean is my lonely looks a lot like insomnia when you hold it up to the light. what i mean is if i came to you, lonely as a grocery store parking lot at 5am, blowing smoke rings but pretending they are halos, could you believe in the magic? not beauty, not the beast, i mean enchanted castle. my body: space jam. my toothy smile has ways to tell anything else than the truth: flight response.   do you ever sit on the end of your bed and listen to the world spin? i hear that song everywhere. when i say that song, what i mean is time. time is a holy catastrophe of heirloom clock faces that don't fit my wrists. the only instrument i know how to play is a muscle. i like my body best when i am not worried about how much space it is taking up. i mean dancing. when i say dancing, i mean shimmy-and-a-shake-and-a-womp-womp-drop. my swagger has moves like it sleeps in a waterbed. i mean my seed sleeps in its shell.   i am best prepared for the worst case scenario. the best case scenario scares me. flight response. my mother tells me i am a bird. when she says i am a bird, she means the whole world is my cage. in my dreams, i can fly, and there is no such thing as a cage, meaning there is no such thing as time. i have been here before. i mean i recognize that moon. i know, there are many moons, and my gratitude eclipses them all. so, i say thank you. thank you when i mean   hello.

it's a pleasure to meet you, reader.
my hope is that this book might be
a friend, a reminder, a testament
that the first step to connection is communication.
thank you & hello…

contents

first date

*

what you see is what you get,
but that's not all there is.

-my grandmother, Jean

hurdles / dreams

new earrings / new ring formation / new kiss goodnight / most week-
ends / still falling asleep / in the middle of the bed / sometimes / i am
/ little lady / who wishes herself a flower / that wishes itself a balloon
/ how i always want to grow / high / get above it / i am / not here / to
look at the dirt / beneath anyone's fingernails / oh / the tricks we use
/ to distract ourselves / how they don't always work / i still dream of
you / sometimes / i wake up / with a basketball inflated / in my chest
/ sitting atop my rack of ribs / waiting / for an invitation / to dribble
/ on your court / of course / at your court/ it's patio weather / like
/ all the time / right / imagine me / sticky as a popsicle stick / with
feelings / all / parched hands & clammy tongue / hungry for a kiss /
then /there is the dream / that reoccurs / the wicked game / where
you pretend / you are a ghost / & i talk to myself / in rooms full of
strangers /or / the impossible dream / where your hand / slips / &
your fingers / weave / easily into mine / or / the one i am inside of
the whale's mouth /i yell out / for you to come join me / "i'm sorry
it's so dark in here" / i tell you / but i am not sorry / for the darkness /
only that it makes you so afraid / or / worst of all / the dream i cannot
seem to wake from / i am jumping days like hurdles / for months &
months & months / to get over you / why do i think it's possible / to
write the bricks out of a wall /why am i banging my head / against a
brick wall / begging / please please please / for a different memory /
one where the lilac wind did not lick my eyelashes / that way / where
i look at you / & in my head Joanna Newsom does not sing / 'you are
starry starry starry' / i know / none of it makes sense / i know / trust
me / there is no sleep for this lonely / no birds / this morning / only
the sound of my upstairs neighbors / making breakfast / at least /
they aren't using the blender / at least / their baby girl isn't crying /
& neither am i / anymore

the slow now

this morning said
            do not press snooze.

                        you pressed snooze
                        but
                        only once
                        congratulations

while brushing your teeth,
your reflection in the mirror also said:
            congratulations.

                        you said
                        thank you
                        out loud
            to every cotton swab in the blue box
            & blue seashell on the shower curtain

you filled your kettle with cold water,
set it on the hot stovetop, to boil
this morning said,
            get dressed.

                        you sat
                        mostly naked
                        on your bed
                        watching YouTube videos
                        of Amy Winehouse
                        singing back to black
                        for thirty-six minutes
            you rummaged through a drawer
                        found a bra
                        put it on

you put on black tights
tried on four dresses
finally decided on the black & white flowers one
nineteen minutes later
you put on a sweater
& you sat
fully dressed
on your bed
for five minutes more

you say hello to afternoon.
afternoon asks
        if you have eaten anything,
        if you plan on leaving the house today.

                you pick up the phone
                        say
                i am starting the pills again
                        tomorrow
                i have a doctor's appointment
                first thing in the morning

your mother responds,
        didn't i tell you to do that two weeks ago?

explaining my depression to my mother
a conversation

mom,
my depression is a shape shifter;
one day it is as small as a firefly in the palm of a bear,
the next, it's the bear.
those days i play dead until the bear leaves me alone.

i call the bad days
the dark days.

    mom says try lighting candles.

when i see a candle, i see the flesh of a church.
the flicker of life sparks a memory younger than noon;
i am standing beside her open casket,
it is the moment i realize every person i ever come to know
will someday die.
besides, mom, i'm not afraid of the dark,
perhaps that is part of the problem.

    mom says i thought the problem was
    that you can't get out of bed?

i can't.
anxiety holds me hostage inside of my house, inside of my head.

    mom says where did anxiety come from?

anxiety is the cousin visiting from out of town
depression felt obligated to bring to the party.
mom, i am the party.
only, i am a party i don't want to be at.

mom says why don't you try going to actual parties?
see your friends.

sure, i make plans.
i make plans but i don't want to go.
i make plans because i know i should want to go,
i know at some point i would have wanted to go,
it's just not that much fun having fun when you don't
want to have fun.

mom,
each night, insomnia sweeps me up into its arms,
dips me in the kitchen by the small glow of stove light.
insomnia has this romantic way of making the moon
feel like perfect company.

    mom says try counting sheep.

my mind can only count reasons to stay awake.

so i go for walks, mom, but
my stuttering kneecaps clank like silver spoons
held in strong arms with loose wrists.
they ring in my ears like clumsy church bells,
reminding me i am sleepwalking on an ocean of happiness
i cannot baptize myself in.

    mom says happy is a decision.

my happy is a high fever that will break.
my happy is as hollow as a pin-pricked egg.

    mom says i am so good at making something out of nothing,
    and then flat out asks me if i am afraid of dying.

no,
i am afraid of living.

mom, i am lonely.
i think i learnt it when dad left;
how to turn the anger into lonely,
the lonely into busy.
when i tell you i've been super busy lately,
i mean i've been falling asleep watching sportscenter on the couch
to avoid confronting the empty side of my bed.

my depression always drags me back to my bed
until my bones are the forgotten fossils of a skeleton sunken city.
my mouth, a boneyard of teeth broken from biting
down on themselves.

the hollow auditorium of my chest swoons with echoes
of a heartbeat, but i am a careless tourist here,
i will never truly know everywhere i have been.

   mom still doesn't understand.

mom,
can't you see?
neither do i.

what i told the doctor

the eyes are not reliable.
not windows. not mirrors.

my ears have eroded,
leaving two broken telephones.

my hands have embraced what they always have been;
two grasping panics, two torches to everything i love.

feet - nothing more than two rocks some days.

& my heart has developed a kind of amnesia,
where it remembers everything but itself.

self(heart)-portrait

honey, yeah, sticky, but
sweetsweetsweet. swollen
sweet home, or
swollen lonely abandoned
house. temporary kingdom,
crown, that is not for keeps.
plump sour cherry. set in the
sun to dry, a dress handed
down from my mother. my
grandmother's finest teacup,
half-full of dust and collecting,
still. fistful of pulse. flightless
balloon. awaiting pop,
or deflate. a fickle framework; i am
a clock i cannot tell.

a story // my father moves to another country &
there's no way to say i'm sorry if you aren't

it's the night before we arrive in San Francisco, which is, so far, my
favorite night of our three week trip. we are somewhere on the coast,
at a Holiday Inn. our room is standard: two beds, a TV, a mini fridge.
we are each sprawled on our bed, atop the covers. you have a con-
ference call with the office in China for work, on our vacation, so we
are staying in for the night. an acceptable consolation: you toss me
a twenty to raid the vending machine. while i stock up on chocolate
bars i think to myself this isn't so bad. while waiting for your call to
come in, we catch a marathon of *The Golden Girls*, and gently into
the evening, like two kettles of boiling water, we are laughing at all
the same parts.

it's tomorrow and we are in San Francisco, finally. after a day of be-
ing holed-up in your car, we're sitting at a patio table at Fisherman's
Wharf. sea salt breeze, i keep licking my lips. we have a whole crab on
the table. you played Grim Reaper and picked him out on the way to
our seats. i'm also tipsy from splitting this bottle of white wine with
you. of course this is cool of you to do: split a bottle of wine with me.
i'm two months shy of my twenty -first birthday. i don't realize din-
ner with you now is much easier than it will be in the future.

looking back, that trip was one of our better ones, if not the best. i
bought my leather jacket on that trip. it's been my main choice in
weather protection for the past seven years.

it's weird…how a jacket can be more reliable than a father.

nature versus nurture

it has been said that i am just like my father.
this might explain why most days,
i dress up in my mother's clothes.
use her signature shade of scarlet to paint my lips a familiar smile.
i do not use her signature trick of turning her heart inside out,
the way she showed me, to wear her softness as bulletproof vest.
armor is for women who have something to lose,
in this way, i am not like my mother;
the inside of my heart is covered in stucco scales.
my father has a crocodile smile -
a flawless flash of shiny distraction to keep you
from finding the bodies he's left behind.
but if you look close enough, the evidence lies
in the residue between his teeth.
i have been told my tongue should come with a warning
of blunt force trauma. it's true, there are nights
i wear nothing but a blood-stained smirk to veil my secrets.
there are nights my smile is the simple act of baring my teeth.
i am just like my father,
and if it weren't for my mother,
i would not know how to take responsibility
for the bite i bear when i wear the crocodile smile.
because there are nights i cannot help myself;
when the full moon howls,
i howl back.
i am the daughter of nature versus nurture.
each verse for my father is a love letter to my mother.
my mother the sparrow.
my mother the nest.
my mother the branches.
my mother the leaves.
my mother the tree who cut and whittled herself to build me
a boat offering safe passage.
my eyes watch our slow sailing reflection in the water.

in its stillness, it's almost impossible to tell
if the tiny yellow lights scattered across its surface are
mirrored stars or crocodile eyes,
but my basic instincts are well acquainted with the sensation
of nature's gaze fixated on me;
when my father tells me i am beautiful,
i always hope it's because i remind him of my mother.

single

    is

         unshaven legs
         same flannel for a week
         not checking in
         not being checked on
         cheese and crackers for dinner
         Skittles bought drunk at 3am for breakfast
         sweatpants
         no pants
         no bra
         clean laundry in a pile at the end of the bed
         chocolate in bed
         movies in bed
         tv in bed
         bad tv in bed
         books in bed
         writing in bed
         texting in bed
         phone calls in bed
         not answering phone calls in bed
         dreaming of not being in bed, in bed

single is everything in bed
everything
but company

the loneliest sweet potato

i am at the grocery store because i feel sad. i feel sad because nobody is in love with me. nobody is in love with me but everybody loves me. everybody loves me because i'm good at making people feel good. i'm good at making people feel good because i have had a lot of practice on myself. practice on myself because i feel sad a lot. i feel sad a lot, but when i make people feel good, i feel good for a little bit. i feel good for a little bit, until i get lonely. i get lonely and i am uncomfortable in my lonely. at the grocery store i practice trying to make myself feel good by pretending i am a regular person buying her groceries & not a very sad person trying to distract herself from crying. crying gives me a headache. headaches make me want to crawl into bed. crawling into bed is what sad people do. what sad people do when they are lonely looks a lot like me at the grocery store. at the grocery store, i feel sad but i look just like everybody else while picking out avocados. or lemons. items no one refers to as comfort food. comfort food makes me want to crawl into bed. crawling into bed reminds me of two things: i am sad & i am alone. i am alone, in the grocery store, moving slow in the condiment aisle. in the condiment aisle important decisions are made & everybody knows it is perfectly acceptable to stand around for too long. stand around for too long & i will begin to tap dance. *tap dance lonely in the condiment aisle is a great title for a book,* i think, as i wait in line to reach the cashier. the cashier seems surprised when i ask her how her night is going. her night is going okay, she says. she says nothing else, except: cash, credit, or debit? she waves goodbye. goodbye is the saddest word i know. the saddest word you know is my name. my name walks around at the grocery store & feels less sad. less sad, because at the grocery store, at least nobody knows there is nobody in love with me.

that awkward moment

when
October
uses his hands
to make shadow puppets
against the supermoon:
a dog…a butterfly…
& all
i can think
is
what is the moon
if not a magician
all i can think
is
the night sky is a lid
with pinholes
all i can think
is
his hands
will never
hold my body
holy
as a prayer
between them.

minnows

i have minnows in my stomach.

i swallowed them singing to you underwater.

you once told me as a child,
you seldom remembered to feed your fish.

my body is a fishbowl i have caught you watching.

you can thank my ballet training for teaching me
how to hold my body
like a champagne flute in the hand of a debutante.

i started drinking again to control my inside tides.
i continue drinking to keep the minnows alive.

i have minnows in my stomach.

at first, i thought they were butterflies.
the butterflies turned out to be your hands making shadows.

remember
that night we fell asleep with the candles burning?
the school of flickering light that swam across the wall -
i imagined i was inside of an aquarium exhibition
featuring the fish inside of you. they were
beautiful.

i have minnows in my stomach.
they are hungry.
starving.

is it that you are forgetful or sadistic?

i have minnows in my stomach that are going to die soon.

i've turned the top two chambers of my heart into a mausoleum
in anticipation. engraved each tiny tombstone with my fingernail,
i gave each fish its own nickname.

—

i had minnows in my stomach.

there is a stillness now.

a small condolence:
their face down float
was the closest they ever came to being
butterflies.

—

it's my twenty-sixth birthday.
he arrives to my quasi-adult potluck dinner party
holding three styrofoam containers of seaweed salad
from the sushi spot
on the corner.

he says:
> *little lady,*
> *i'm sorry it took me so long to get here.*
> *i hope i'm not too late for the party.*

better together
a Jack Johnson erasure

I believe in memories

But there is not enough time

magic trick 001

the girl gets carried away.

she is the sugar cube,
love is the cup of
darjeeling - she
dissolves,
faster
than
you
think
she
will.

(i)

i drink my coffee black. every morning. i like how looking at you
makes me feel. twice i asked to kiss you. the second time, there was
a lump in my throat. i like to believe it was a metaphor. a plain
tumor is all it was. i have woken up
looked in the mirror & thought damn i look good
today. if i am late it is because i don't know
how to plan time.

cut to me blushing. laughing, of course. we were
no full moon. in my poems you are the dream of you.
the falling stars are just glitter just thousands of tiny LED lights
poured down from the sky. that July was a fire that minded its own
business. the following June was just thirty days the moon was
a strawberry. it wasn't the drugs the shadows on the ceiling
weren't dancing again.

i was walking backwards when i met you. you are not the first
boy who i wrote into existence, or loved.
that thought unties my shoelaces.

once, we were a crescent moon, weightless as a smile.

i love you. still. i'm not sorry. i don't want to write about you any-
more. let's see how long we can go without talking. this time,
if we really try, maybe i will forget your birthday. i miss you, but
i don't wish you were here.

(ii)

you don't like coffee. you like what it does to your body,
you like the way coffee makes your body feel. so you take your cream
& sugar with coffee. i'm not sure why you kissed me back
the first time. i suspect you
liked what it did to your body; you
liked the way my kiss made your body
feel. once. i let you wrap your palms around my neck
to feel the tumor ride my throat like an elevator.

you wear sweat shorts & i still want to fuck you. once.
you gave me a bouquet of pink roses or was it a fury of
your puckered lips? when your elbow found mine in that crowd
after a year of our mouths not speaking i was not happy to see you i was
relieved. once you said a person is either
a peacekeeper or a pot stirrer. we both know
which i am. i bet you think you're a peacekeeper. i bet
you think magicians don't exist.

you are the first dizzy wind spell to trip my tornado.
once, you smiled in my direction & balloon on the loose
there i went so high i forgot which came first you or the dream
of you.

you told me, once, after work, you took the bus all the way
west to watch the sunset, only to miss it. you said
you were so glad you made it to me on time.

if you came back, i would not ask why.
you may say none of this ever happened.

so, I'm talking to depression...

& i'm like blah blah blah whatever sabrina
who? i am whatever you last called me in my head
y'know? except i'm not nothing
i have a heavy pulse which is a kind
of thing like a zip a dee doo dah
between my orgasms i try not to cry i laugh
at all the jokes my friends say to me on my birthday
i ask my grandmother for an apple pie i draw
a lot of lines they don't mean a thing to you
you are an invisible bone that i
caught & can't stop writing poems about
i mean living (ha!) i am
the strangest of days same as you
who cares i'm just trying to be less predictable
anyway you slip me a fog you are molasses
or something like molasses whatever i am
softer than i think you are even if i have
a mouth like a smoking
gun that does not
know where
the bullets
went

girl beside you

the girl sitting
diagonally
across from me
on the subway
          let's call her curly hair
is carrying
a small bouquet
of lavender
wrapped in
brown paper
held together
by a neat twine bow

curly hair is watching
the girl standing
diagonally
across from her
          let's call her crimson lipstick
do the crossword

crimson lipstick is wearing
headphones
& holding
an enviable focus
in her eyes
which are
entirely absorbed
in the puzzle

sitting
curly hair
with the purple flowers
has sad ladybug eyes

& each time
we reach a station
they search
frantically
the platform
of waiting-to-be-passengers

curly hair gets off the train
with crimson lipstick
at the same
stop
they never
make eye contact

       i don't know how to connect in a world like this;
       in times like these,
       where i can't even speak about myself in first person.

a plain truth

on the days i wake up
& my name is a euphemism
for depressed, or anxious, or whatever;
i drink my coffee while the inanimate objects
in my apartment talk at me.
i do not try to make out anything they are saying.
i cannot tell you the number of times i put my hair up
into a bun only to take it right back down
because i am afraid of the kink the elastic will leave. it's
exhausting. what they don't tell you about self-care,
that it can make you feel like you are the coach,
the captain, & every.other.player.
oh, & the mascot.
it can make you feel especially like the mascot.

magic trick 002

the girl learns to fly.

she is a fish.
the hook is in the water.
she willingly thrusts her body onto the hook
all for a better look at the stars.

dear Beyoncé (I)

why is it all so heavy...why does my heart insist on being a carriage of arms...happiness a bag of sugar too big for my bird bones...will Kentucky always be there...a folded faded love note in my every back pocket...put my pen to paper the first thing to come out is yesterday's name...the inelegant haunt of memory...i just want to be free... is it okay if my definition of free is yet to be determined...when the sky fell...you would think i would have run...i stood cemented in the relief there was nowhere else to go...is that freedom...is sleep time travel...is time a sleeping language...will time tell...why are our bodies sandcastle clocks built with hands in perpetual prayer to slow the dissolve of time...do the clocks know their only job is to evenly measure out our lifespans...do the stars know they are ghosts the way we know we might never be...& where are our wings...

how to unfold a memory // the kentucky heartbreak shuffle

a wink & a crooked smile. chorus of cracking knuckles: a concert of injuries. the fireflies, bats, June bugs, & i; we all saw you watching. the crickets chirped grateful for the angel's share, like *gawdamn, this air tastes delicious.*

speaking of bourbon, Kentucky was barrels on barrels. cornmeal fried catfish, clocks with roman numerals, & the street lamps. ooh, the street lamps. wrap around porches, the porch swings, the American flag - i know, there is nothing romantic about colonialism, but there was something about the architecture that whispered secret sticky sweet nothings. i was stuck in the roundabout. i was inside looking out, finally.

see, i had been going in circles swallowing words. dizzy, i had to lie down before the church. at midnight, i had to lay time flat & still the treetops. fireflies, bats, June bugs & i, we all stood watching the ghost ships of light sail the sea-sky.

silent treatment: the fantastic devastation of unwanted silence. that heavy slink; how it hangs with purpose; mean, easy. my tongue, well trained in the sit-still,
it's my hands that can't keep a secret. my legs, too eager to run into the music,

i went looking for our bridge to burn. & a river bank to drown the flames, stifle the heat. Kentucky was hot; all bare foot & blue flame. i wouldn't say i could see the music, but the music could see me; bare bone wind chime. bare skin dunked in: swimming pool day dreams. full moon feelings. that can't take my eyes off of you. the sticky hands of lust tip-toeing earthquake. it was always & never the right time.

one might have found me akin to a scoop of ice cream atop soda pop bubbles: light as air, without care for the impending melt.

i plucked a daisy in Kentucky. it told me that you loved me. i left your love there. there in the dancing around, dancing through, dancing on the spot where i buried my expectations. & the wanting of it all. the truth hurts less when it is not parading around in front of us. love, that great & terrible handsome beast, trace me back to it by a trail of smoke.

i only doused myself in gasoline when you handed me that match because i was tired of being a metaphor. why is it
always about burning?

in Kentucky, there is a pile of bricks where a bridge could not measure the space between us.

there is a condition called the rapture of the deep. it occurs when a deep sea diver spends too much time at the bottom of the ocean & cannot tell which way is up. you have always been asleep in a different bed in the same room. Kentucky felt like
impossible nostalgia.

i saw you looking back.

i remember i saw you looking back because i was

looking forward.

my jaw was a clenched fist i could not throw. the truth hurts loudest when you toss it around,
& the echo…the echo is what drives girls like me

mad with remembering.

house of cards
a Radiohead erasure

I don't wanna be
                your lover
          how it ends

Forget about

           the table

The   collapse

        your keys in the
Kiss   good night
Forget   your house
          mine
          your house
&   mine

          be burning

how to fold a memory

>our brains remember the infliction
>of pain, be it physical, psychological, or emotional.
>we remember this hurt as a means to avoid it in the future.

let's start at the beginning.
i remember the shape my hand held while in yours,
like origami prayer, or flower petals returning home.
i remember the rose petals falling from your fingers,
leading from the doorway to the bedroom like a
trail of breadcrumbs, or drops of blood.
the scent of cinnamon, how you would sprinkle it into my coffee
like fresh ground snowflakes.
i can't take cinnamon in my coffee
without getting hungry for your laughter.
i am hungry for your laughter, but my mouth tastes like the slow
dissolve of the last i love you that refused to leave it.
i remember the river. how we danced to the sound of it rushing.
how you hummed Radiohead in harmony.
that song haunts my house of cards. i wish it would collapse.
i wish i could forget how i got here.
how did i get here? i was carried in the teeth
of your charm, or i walked.
i marched. i was a turning cheek parade.
i wasn't paying attention to the highlighted route,
or there was no map, i got lost.

>with every journey back into our past, it becomes harder
>to find our way there.
>our brains are constantly rerouting the paths, rewriting
>what we remember.

let's go to the end -
it was by Little Sugar Creek, in the warm Kentucky breeze,
we stood off unfolding in silence.
in silence, it's hard to tell what the other person

is thinking without looking them in the eyes.
you would not look me in the eyes.
so, by Little Sugar Creek, i let the warm breeze reach
you in place of my origami hands.

ever since, i have been practicing forgetting.
i've kissed the sky more times than i ever kissed you.
i inhale purple haze in an attempt to smoke out the correlation
between you & the scent of cinnamon.
i drink as if i am trying to save the world from drowning.
to get my memories so drunk,
they might forget themselves by morning.
but the trauma of daydreaming.
the curse of muscle memory; my body keeps your secrets.

how do i teach my mouth to shake out the reflection
of your etch-a-sketch smile?
my wrists, to forget the swoops and arcs of your name?
my ears, to hear songs without the ghost of you inside of them?

worse, i cannot tell in these spasms of remembering,
if the past tense keeps slipping into my present,
or if my present keeps slipping into the past.
still, my body wears your fingerprints like a home address.
 i lose memories like baby teeth, but you
are a stubborn molar refusing to leave.

> we cannot control what we remember,
> but we can control how we remember.

i shake cinnamon into my coffee, & i don't think of you.
i write your name over & over, until it no longer has any meaning.
i fold my memories of you, craft them paper wings,
in hopes they might one day drift into amnesia,
& you might leave me,
without a trace.

gravity speaks

> if i am holding you without hands,
> how am i supposed to let go?

the other side of a memory

we could have told you
she wasn't herself since the tenth grade
sure, she still had a laugh like electricity
still went to dance class
put on mascara each morning for school
but something was off
something like how a light switch will still turn on
a half burnt bulb
it was hard to tell if she was a stubborn surge
or a tired, dimming circuit
then she started working weekends
stopped making it for dinner on Sundays
when she did she looked exhausted
but she was always missing our calls
telling us she had been asleep
she had never been one to lie
so we believed her
we wanted to believe her when she said she was fine
just fine / all right / okay / busy / good / okay / fine
we thought she would have come to us
if she was having any trouble we would have done anything
to help
all we've ever wanted was for her to be happy

for my nineteenth birthday, my brother gifted me the
board game hungry hungry hippos,
he said it was so i could play with my friends.
he was referring to the hippos.

we did not understand why she would not stop crying
even when we held her down to the couch begging her to

35

on releasing light

in some stories,
the protagonist has to kill the bad thing to release its light.

in my story,
i am the protagonist & the bad thing,
i have to learn how to bend the light out of myself.

                                                    i can do that magic.

magic trick 003

the girl performs her first spell.

during a fit of anger, she breaks
her own heart in a parking lot at Disneyland as her father watches on.
inside of her heart was a skipping stone,
the heart pieces assemble into a tiny hummingbird that flies
back into the girl's chest,
but it metabolizes her love so quickly,
it is always moments away from starving to death.

poem from last august california trip //
yearly maintenance

the notice taped to the door
said:
> **everything off the counters.**

so we took everything off.

> *the coffee maker*
> *olive oil*
> *blame*

& take a look at all this grey speckled marble;
so smooth,
unlike our fitful conversations.

> *a blender*
> *the cutting board*

don't worry -
the knives are kept in drawers:

> *three sets of keys*

hers,
& father's,
& mine are father's too.

> *two loaves of bread*
> *a box of tea*

step-mother drinks tea,
& father drinks coffee,
& i drink father's coffee too.
it's all hot under the surface.

> *a small watermelon*

father cuts me off mid-sentence,

> *the toaster*

unplugged but still warm.
once we've finished,
father turns on the tv.
he puts on something funny

so we can laugh,
& laugh,
& forget
we'll have to put everything back tomorrow;
where we keep it, where it all goes.

i press shuffle & Lauryn Hill comes on...

& all of a sudden
i am standing in
a June
some twenty-six moons ago
losing my bravery
in the maze
something about
the walls
being too white
& how neither of us
reach
for the purple crayons
scattered like dares
in the dry grass
we are silent
the whole walk
i'm thinking
about why i didn't do it
we stay silent
while moving smoothly
through mundane interactions
as if routine
that night
i did not ask
& you did not tell
but Lauryn Hill sang
nothing even matters
& we both
sang along
we both sang
out loud
nothing but you

another plain truth

we hugged.
it was a good hug.
if there is such a thing as a hug so good i did not wish it were a kiss.

on the last gesture between us

so / i guess you could say / it wasn't that bad / & i might be inclined to believe you / except / i know things / that i can't explain / that make me almost positive / a wave goodbye / on a full moon / means / let go / & go home / & so i went / quietly into the night / with my swallow / & the Uber driver was very nice / turned around & introduced himself to me / told me i looked like a jazz girl & tuned the radio stations until the syrupy leak of trumpet sweetened both of our lips into smiles / & then he said here you go & turned it up / & i was grateful for this stranger who understood me / who asked of me nothing /left as much empty space in that silver sedan as he could for the music / the medicine / i opened my mouth to say thank you / but the thick wail of saxophone slid down my throat / & again / quietly / i swallowed my cry / into song / my cry / an instrumental mourning/ the words / the words they are always changing /a wave goodbye / is always a mocking lifeline / & i guess you could say /my dark purple lipstick distraction plan would have worked / if i hadn't worn my reaction like too-thick black winged eyeliner that doesn't suit my face / but it's fine / because i look like a jazz girl / & right now / eyes closed & tears streaming & a little tipsy letsbehonest / i am a jazz girl / a girl of pulled taffy / a girl who will chew / a wave goodbye / for weeks / before spitting it out / onto a page / into a song / titled: i think i'll prefer you a stranger someday.

poem from the moment after you left
for chimwemwe

& the truth is
i miss you already
the truth is
you're still here
in my heart
the truth is
we never truly know
if or where we will be
together again
but i look forward
with wide open arms
to that next time
when we find ourselves
sharing the glow we keep
instead of cavities in our teeth
& joking about time
how its passing
is nothing more
than a dream
how we are
never more
than a short slumber
away

on platonic love being a real thing

while drinking pear cider / on **E**'s rooftop / for **K**'s birthday / **S** asks / do *you remember your first kiss / i laugh / yes / of course / it was during a game of spin the bottle / look / he is sitting across from us / at this table /* right now / **A** senses our attention / looks at me / mid-bite of his hamburger / pulls it out of his mouth / & opens up / showing the product of his chewing / all three of us laugh / **S** says: i totally get it / i think about that game of spin the bottle / how **A** was the only boy to come to my grade seven birthday party / how we still played spin the bottle / & all kissed whoever it landed on / i think about how **E** was my prom date & the first girl i kissed with tongue / how that kiss was actually a secret pact to make me promise not to tell **H** that **E** was smoking / & that same night we slept over at **H**'s house / **K** & i shared a bed / & she took off her shirt / & bra / before she got in / so i did too / & it was no thing / that time **S** & i spent a night laughing naked / i think about each relationship sitting at the table / how we trust each other / with our whole bodies / how that's love / now, isn't that love?

so my friend tells me she identifies as a mermaid...

& i'm like, GIRL. i saw *The Little Mermaid*. even she did not want to be a mermaid. & yes, she may have been a selfish little fishtail, but think about it: "up where they walk, up where they run, up where they play all day in the sun." i mean...don't you currently enjoy doing all of those things? if you're just trying to sing & brush your hair with a fork without judgment, you can totally do that. some people will throw you the side eye, disregard them as crabs. OR are you just trying to say you're magic, BUT not that regular, pedestrian, witch-type magic. is mermaid magic better? is this common public knowledge? OR is it just easier to look at yourself in the mirror if you are not human. does that make it easier to pretend you don't have depression; because depression is exclusively human. if so...shoot...maybe i am a mermaid too. if being a mermaid means you've cried enough tears to drown your grasp of reality. if being a mermaid means you truly believe the grass is greener than the blue you are surrounded by. if being a mermaid means you never walk away from a person you love, because you can't, because you have a fin. then yes, i think i am definitely a mermaid. & every song i've ever sung has filled my lungs with sea, but i am not drowning - not like i thought i was, when i was   human.

avowal

i drink my coffee black. you don't like coffee. you like what it does to your body, you like the way coffee makes your body feel. so you take your cream & sugar with coffee, every morning. **this is not about you.** i like how looking at you makes me feel twice i asked to kiss you the second time, **how you said i just don't think i can give you what you want.** i'm not sure why you kissed me back the first time. i suspect you liked what it did to your body, you liked the way my kiss made your body feel. once, there was a lump in my throat. i like to believe it was a metaphor. **every feeling i have swallowed.** a plain tumor is all it was.

see how this is my story. i have woken up looked in the mirror & thought damn i look good today. you wear sweat shorts & i still want to fuck you. once. you gave me a bouquet of pink roses or was it a fury of your puckered lips? if i am late it is because **i was too anxious to leave.** i don't know how to plan time. when your elbow found mine in that crowd after a year of our mouths not speaking i was not happy to see you i was relieved.

cut to me blushing. laughing, of course. **weren't you dancing beside me?** we were no full moon. once you said a person is either a peace-keeper or a pot stirrer. we both know which i am. i bet you think you're a peacekeeper. in my poems you are the dream of you. **maybe is an alternate universe.** the falling stars are just glitter just thousands of tiny LED lights poured down from the sky that July was a fire that minded its own business the following June was just thirty days the moon was a strawberry it wasn't the drugs the shadows on the ceiling weren't dancing again.

i was walking backwards when i met you. **i made all of this magic.** i bet you think magicians don't exist. you are not the first boy who i wrote into existence, or loved. you are the first dizzy wind spell to trip my tornado. once, you smiled in my direction & balloon on the loose there i went so high i forgot which came first you or the dream of you. that thought unties my shoelaces.

once, we were a crescent moon, weightless as a smile.

you told me, once, after work you took the bus all the way west to watch the sunset, only to miss it. you said you were so glad you made it to me on time. i love you. still. i'm not sorry. i don't want to write about you anymore. let's see how long we can go without talking. this time, if we really try, maybe i will forget your birthday. **maybe**. if you came back, i would not ask why. i miss you, but i don't wish you were here. you may say none of this ever happened. **but some of the details sure fit.***

*abracadabra

on keeping your damn feelings to your damn self

how do you do that?
but also can you just stop.it.right.now.

unrequited *in nine acts*

the question hangs / a hook through my pink cheek:
how did you do that thing that you did to my heart?

\-

because isn't the real tragedy
how you found yourselves in one another,
how you took one brief look into the mirror of her,
turned around,
& walked away?

\-

the girl's arms are empty.
her fists are filled with the laughter of ghosts.
watch their fitful ridicule each time she cries over love
less real than they are.

\-

there are baseballs / falling out of my mouth / each ball / the name of
a body / i reached for in the dark / to find myself / a parade of honest
names / slip / from the grip of my loose glove jaw / the love i want is
a basketball / a heavy thumping / in the chest / when it is my turn to
be called up to the plate / i do not swing / i do not swing

\-

her name is wooden ship, to try & fit in
into his glass bottle heart would only break her.

\-

a montage of all the times i wished you had taken my hand
& when the moment passed
& you didn't,
a montage of all the places i wished myself far, far away to:
Portland, Barcelona, places i have never seen your smile.

-

what is the name of a place that everyone can see is burning...but no
one can feel the effects of the smoke...or the heat of the flames...
except the place...& that place is not a place but a person...& that
person is the i in my poems...only it's my real life body that aches...&
isn't that love...not being able to see the explosion... because you are
the one holding the bomb...& the bomb is also you

-

the girl's hair turns to forget-me-nots and thyme.
her bones soften to willow branches, her skin flakes maple leaves.
her chest is now a cabinet of well-stacked cigar box caskets
carrying memories she is slow turning to ash. in lieu of conversation,
she passes smoke.

the girl collects seashells, upturns them into bowls, fills them
with dried lavender & amethyst, in hopes
of luring someone new.
remembering is her favorite pastime.
she cannot hold her heart up without trembling, so she hides it
away in bottomless midnights, which are her grief, but are also her lust.
the girl is now a girl who is also a whale; full of unoccupied space.
it's tragic how she displaces her emptiness with loneliness,
how she wants & wants & wants & needs to know why.
why the boy acts like he lives so far away from her
when his house is just a couple blocks south of ten
minutes & all that space lays still, loud as a snail's cry.

& wouldn't i know about crawling up inside oneself
wouldn't i know about a body full of waiting
a floor, clean as a plate in a cupboard, holding nine other plates
on top of it
how it's all so unbearable
holding love makes the girl feel helpless. she dislikes the period of
heavy pockets, of change her heart is
unwilling to make.

-

did you hear me?
i said i love you.
i said i still love you.
still. you.

dear Beyoncé (II)

why is it all so heavy...i of course mean my heart...but can i call it a
heart if it has the reluctant tenderness of a blackberry...i slouch to-
ward the window...i sit in the dark until someone comes in the room
& turns on the light...what does it mean that i imagine my heart is
a stampede of trembling rabbits...& why do i prefer hands to eyes...
the hunger for a warm pulse...what is more savage than that kind of
loneliness...i have kissed love on the lips & it did not fill me with
anything other than smoke...what if the place where i keep my love is
a cave...cluttered with mumbling grief...what if my heart only prays
in the church of a mouth... & how can you believe in yourself to tell
the truth when a lover asks you what you are afraid of...the more i
come to know about snakes the better i understand...i am terrified
of myself...i leave my skin all over the place...i am always digesting
my last meal...

feed a fever, starve a cold

to forget
the artichoke heart
buries itself in leaves
to the source of the true hunger
to look full
to appear flush
*
my grandmother says
heartache is
a hungry caterpillar
that must be fed
so it can grow
wings
& fly away
*
the refusal of offered love
is some kind of death
*
to forget
the warmth of a smile
when it was smiling
at me
i wear scarves
& toques
before
the snow comes
i call this
being prepared
i am just
lonely
*
my heart
believes
his smile's last words

were a secret handshake
i have not eaten dessert
since
*

if the bag
of carrot sticks
is full
i do not bother
counting
how many i eat
there are never enough
*

when my friend
tells me
i seem
smaller
i joke
i am
too young
to be
shrinking
when he says
no sabrina,
i mean
skinnier
& i tell him
not on purpose
i am not lying
*

i tell
my grandmother
i think love is
a hungry caterpillar
*

i am no meal
historically
i have never been
more
than a midnight
snack

poem from the beach trip

i ask why the birds are crying & learn that seabirds drink salt water
& then cry out the salt through their tears & though i cannot say for
sure i believe this to suggest the seabirds aren't sad they are excel-
lent at letting go cool i have woken up & cried for three mornings in
a row each time felt as if there was a reason but i could not remem-
ber it i was hoping the seabirds might relate as i watch them fly my
bones feel so heavy the tide is coming in & a bright moon crab digs
bunkers into the sand to wait out the wave & the wave is endless &
there are waves & waves & i am clutching my entire body tense as
the moment you ask me what happened why am i crying again & the
best answer i can give you is i can't tell if the crab is still there

girl behind you

girl behind you / at the hardware store / carrying an item you're sure i don't know how to use by myself / & it mildly annoys me / that that's not entirely untrue / my grandfather showed me how / but i will still YouTube a tutorial when i get home / anyway / i'm in line behind you at the grocery store / & i'm carrying the healthy variety of food that needs to be cooked for consumption & you are thinking to yourself / can this small girl really be buying these vegetables & spices for her household or is her mom waiting in the car / & it mildly excites me that i'm thinking i hope my boyfriend is taking a shower / i hope i get home somehow perfectly timed to his exit from the shower / & when i walk in the house /he walks out of the bathroom / & our eyes lock / our lips curl in canary smirks / & 5 minutes later / i am out of breath against the hallway / instead of evenly chopping cubes of sweet potato / but i'm in line behind you at Shoppers Drug Mart / or Walgreens / or wherever you go for toothpaste & condoms / & you are wondering why i am buying vitamins & not lipstick / you are wondering why my nails aren't painted but i'm buying nail polish remover / you are making strange assumptions based on the unkept nature of my frizzy-ass hair / & this is why i have a hard time leaving the house / this is why i didn't braid my hair or put it up into a ponytail / even though that would have made me more comfortable physically / i just knew it would make me appear even younger than i already do / & you're thinking who cares / looking young is great / you're gonna love that you look seventeen when you're thirty / quit whining about a problem that's not really a problem / & this is why i have a hard time talking about my anxieties / not the big heavy anxieties /but the small ones / the ones that change my earrings / & chip at my general level of self-esteem / the ones that gorge on celery & watermelon after a heavy weekend / crying quietly / standing in line / behind you / the girl you're pretending not to notice

what i told the doctor, the second time

everything is in slow motion   again.
              breath the pace of an afternoon walk against the wind.
              heart pulses like dormant volcano.

oscillating head.

                       my thoughts are spirographs;
think intricate patterns of loops,
                       think waves that never break.
   my feet are two bowling balls headed toward the same strike,
but the lane
keeps
growing   &   growing.
  my eyes have formed a reckless search party.
          there is snow in the window but i see cotton balls on string.
each moment hangs in the air around me
                   a poem waiting to be plucked.
if i bite my tongue my mouth bleeds shark bait.
               when i sit still my thoughts circle me
when i want to be left alone
                  i go out into the world.
        in the center of me hangs a small bell,
  i don't know how to ring it,
                  but i've heard it ring.
      i can't stop thinking about when it will ring next

last Friday

lately / my mind has been
spinning the question / what
if i am the sound the tree makes
when it falls in the forest & no
one is around / but i think it's more
likely that i am the no one / deaf to
the libraries falling all around me /
something like fifty-five million people
die / this year / so many stars
shot off into the darkness / & i'm trying
not to entertain these thoughts / on
the weekends / at least / tonight / my
friends & i / we sit around wooden
tables listening / to music made by musicians
who will never play these songs again / &
we only sing along to yesterday's living / until
the record stops / & no one gets up to turn it
over / & someone shouts *hey! did i already tell you*
that i saw a shooting star last night? / & we talk
about how much we adore shooting stars / we
recall the coordinates of the last time
we each have seen one / like they are
some kind of collection of all our lost earrings /
elegant glistening we will never witness in the
light again / & before the conversation spins out /
i get up & flip the vinyl / my step-father
gave to me / so i wouldn't have to inherit it /
someday / & i am grateful for that.

seven small ways in which
i loved myself this week

i flossed.
*
while picking up fruit
& vegetables
at the market,
i
spontaneously
bought myself
flowers.
*
i practiced saying i love you
in the mirror.
not i love you because,
or,
i love you despite,
just:
i love you.
*
it rained,
i went for a walk &
did not bring
an umbrella.
& while my wet hair
reached for the ground
i kept my chin up,
i kept my eyes open.
*
i indulged in a donut
for breakfast
& did not step on a scale
afterward.
*

i held hands
with my sadness,
sang it songs in the shower,
fed it lunch,
got it drunk
& put it to bed early.
*
i did not think
of him.
not even once.

ode to sunday

dreams of kissing,
croissants come true.
this morning
sun, a full joy.
morning glories brave sprout through wood steps.
today slowly finds its balance
and it is here,
in the unsteady,
i find myself
for a moment
writing love letters
and lazy praise
to the calm wide open

***

you clean break / you swift waltz of untangling knots
you cathedral of roses / stop pinching your thorns
you damp wood / miracle / you / crackling campfire
you nervous firework
welcome yourself / back into yourself
you are a playground for dancing ghosts
you are unassuming music
you are dripping faucet / easy tears / winding river
you maple syrup tongue
how do you even talk about anything other than how sweet you are
you with your carousel of questions
you playground for dreams / & new dreams
you moon sugar / you honey cruller lullaby
look at you / sitting in the dark / unfolding
you nesting doll / you kind depth / you terrified bloom
look at all of this digging
look how you have chipped away at your nail polish / both hands
thought you had a garden / but it is a graveyard
so what / if you carry it / under your tongue

magic trick 004

the girl transforms nerves into charm.

"it was a please to meet you."
"a pretty please," she responds.

it starts

with a spark that makes static electricity look like longing.
i am spellbound by the smoke billowing from his Belmont cigarette.
like i am staring at his Belmont cigarette sat
snug between his lips like i wish my name
would. he is so cool. he is like the king of ice cream sandwiches.
like i wish my tongue was a drawbridge to his castle.
his heart is a stubborn pistachio. like i want to crack it open.
i want to play his heartstrings like a harp,
or rip out his heartstrings & like braid them into a bracelet.
like decorate me. i want to wear him.

since i met you baby
a Black Joe Lewis & The Honeybears erasure

    I

                tell

    everybody

         the   doctor

    is you

seconds after bumping into him on the street

there it is,
the bite of nostalgia bleeding.
how painful.
how painfully quick.

on getting over you for real

i recognized you by your shadow   the spill of light from your
outline here is a love poem   more important than the words i
never said   how could i try to make you feel   greener than my
side of the story   this time   i would tell you the deep
truth   which is to say i would take you back into that maze   just
to kiss you   when you were most confused   where i could have
been the one   to make it clear love   can live anywhere   as
long as you acknowledge it   Whitney Houston forced me to
acknowledge   it in a dream   long after she had died & there are
ghosts in every version of this story   dreams that tell like fortunes
& cookies that seem to have fell from the sky   something
like a song link via text message   only there is no mystery
there   except *why*   & little would that matter now in
the terminal of an airport i am only passing through
an aesthetic of clean white tiles & it reminds me of that maze & it helps
me to understand   it's not that i was afraid to write the words
on the wall   it was the shadows they would paint upon our clean
blank   friendship   & again i think *what has not been can never
be lost* too tempting a romance   a beautiful ice sculpture swan   but
how many times has my heart melted   & aren't you so tired of the
chipping away from loneliness' sharp edge each winter   & there
are too many perfect metaphors   for the indie movie i'll keep
on dreaming of writing i would write us wonderful & calm
though i know i wasn't i was anxious & nervous &   horribly
enthusiastic while far too involved in every moment   &you were
casual you were unaware   & who cares   i am in the sky
now   a shadow proving itself to be true a star a manifestation of
the words that describe the feelings i have   moving far inside of
me   & that is how i know   it was real
i walked right into it   into its neon center   &
back out with too many muscles clutching memories of dancing
i bet your best memory of me gets no more attention than a smile
in your sleep   & so it goes   i don't care   i am just happy to
know you   still smile   happy to know   i'll see you around

magic trick 005

the girl lassos a shooting star.

she dissects its gooey center and finds a skipping stone
the girl sits down in a field of grass & stares at the stone for three years
until on the last day of one November it finally snows
& her mother calls her inside
& to hide it safe the girl swallows the stone
                    & it skips
                            on & on
                                    inside her & further away
                                        on & on...

follow-up *a prayer / a spell*

i am feeling better
so i say / good morning / & mean it

yes / today / is a good morning
to exhale / to feel joy

with the release of breath
i no longer need to be holding

i am not alone
because i feel alone

i am not alone because i feel alone
i am not alone because i feel alone / with company

when i look in the mirror i will find a reflection
of the gifts i am withholding from myself

light hits / everything at a different angle
i make a habit of tilting / my head

when the sadness waterfalls
i will let the salt cleanse the wounds i cannot see

i will let dance parties be the hospitals i heal in
if i need more help i will let the people offering help me

if i need more help i will let the medication help me
i forgive my body for being a machine after all

i forgive my memory for being
the cupboard door

that will continue to pop ajar
no matter how many times i push it shut

i forgive myself even if i am the last person i want to forgive
whatever i have come from / wherever i am going

i will remember the present as the place to start
today is a good day / to wake up / & be great

& have gratitude / for the relentless
pump of this heart / the way it does not know how
to hold back
i exhale / & i begin

acknowledgments

first & forever: Santina/mamabear, Jimmy/pops & Jesse. my step-father Tony. my stepmotherfriend Danielle - this collection would not be possible without the lifetime we have spent learning how to love each other. thank you for your patience. // Nanny & Papa: thank you for providing me with an unwavering foundation. Meme: thank you for showing me what it is to be a resilient woman. my grand-father Jack & Nonna G live in my fondest memories. // my many aunts, uncles & cousins of The Sunday Dinner Crew, The Friday Dinner Crew & The Nonna G's Crew, with special thanks to Uncle Sam, the Diagon Palleys & my girl, Victoria. // my second parents, Lina & Ralph, The Fabulous Ladies of Yolo & Donna: you have each been profound influences.

the good folks of Button Poetry: Sam, Dylan, Riley, Nikki, Sarah, Bernard...thank you thank you thank you!!! for believing in me, for believing in my work & for really making my dreams come true. y'all are the best. // Hanif Abdurraqib - to have had you on my side for this journey was a true blessing. you are a gift to this world.

my very good friends: Shane, Cameron, Emma, Holly, Katherine, Matthew, Michael, Arjun, Jill, Greg, Christian, Madeline, Kathryn, Mandee, Steph, & my soulmate Chimwemwe Undi...there are not enough words, so let's just dance until we're old & grey. // Amanda, Kristin, Viktoria & Marlo: thank you for nurturing my writing in the early days. without your support then, i don't know where i would be now. // to the revolving members of The Roo Crew (big love to Sarah, Jared, & Shane): thank you for the last 8 years of sharing magic. // A Big Thank You to Ryan for teaching me to throw a bullseye.

the Canadian spoken word poetry community, with special thanks to these glowing hearts within it: Ian Keteku - GT!!! Andrea Thompson, Britta B, Missy Peters & Dave Morris, Brendan McLeod, Andre Prefontaine, Matt 'LipBalm' Miller, Estefania 'yes' Alfonso, Aaron Simm, Brendan Flaherty, Harriet Wilder, Isaac Bond, Brad Morden, Jillian Christmas, Duncan Shields, Tasha Receno, Erin-Brooke Kirsh, Sean McGarragle, Emilee Nimetz #doublepirouette, Chris Gilpin, Dana ID Matthews, Sonya Littlejohn, Dia Davina, Matt Loeb, Johnny Macrae, Shayne avec-i-grec, Mitcholos Touchie, ƛaphspàtúnak ʔi ƛiṁaqs - ti, Scott Thompson, Colin Michael Matty, Steve Currie, Liam Coady, Erin Dingle, Sheri D Wilson, Tanya Evanson, Mary Pinkoski, Nasra Adem, Nisha Patel, Ahmad Knowmadic Ali, Kaz Mega, Alasdair, Danielle Altrogge, D'J, Mike Johnson, Rabbit Richards, El Jones, Andre Fenton, Rebecca Lea Thomas, Deidre Lee, Khaleefa 'Apollo The Child' Hamdan, Blue, Billy The Kid, Nina Vuleta, Kay Kassirer, DMP, Jamaal Jackson Rogers, Alessandra Naccarato, Elyse Maltin, Jen Slade, Alyssa Ginsberg, Charlie C Petch, Dave Silverberg, Tomy Bewick, Anto Chan, Ifrah Hussien, Holly Painter, The Ragdolls, Rose Jang, Niambi Leigh!!! Toronto Poetry Slam, Wordspell, The Supermarket, The Drake, Avery the Bartender, & last but certainly not least, honorary Canadian Mighty Mike Mcgee - Thank you for accepting my friendship bracelets, for holding space & stages for my work in its many forms, for playing at VFSW, but mostly for graciously giving your time, your energy, your support & your work, which all have moved me to be better in every way.

Rest In Power Zaccheus Jackson Nyce.

in an effort not to list 10,000 more poets, please forgive me for saying that if we are Facebook friends & you are a poet then I would like to thank YOU for the necessary & inspiring work you do. honorable mention to Rudy Francisco for being a real friend since early on in this wild ride.

in no particular order I'd like to take a moment to show gratitude to the following: Beyoncé. bobby pins. peanut m&ms. the moon. coffee. Seawitch fish & chips. the tv show Steven Universe. flowers. fast-moving clouds. coconut water. Whitney Houston. the state of Kentucky. John Mayer. Moleskin notebooks. doctors. grey t-shirts. the movie Eternal Sunshine of the Spotless Mind. rocks, especially quartz. my favorite mug with Zac Efron's face on it. green juice. bonnaroo. Timbits. blue pens. headphones. a polka dot backpack. baggy jeans. trees. peppermint tea. cooking shows of all kinds. books. Ford Escapes. crispy m&ms. bananas. the Toronto Blue Jays. the TTC. mini dachshunds. the internet. Jimmy's Coffee. & baristas everywhere.

to the boys who did not love me back: thank you for the inspiration. // with an extra special shout out to CS whose friendship is pretty cool.

to you, the reader, thank you for taking the time to listen, understand, grieve, remember, learn & love, with me. i am a well of bottomless gratitude. i am carebear-staring it toward you. we are never truly as alone as we feel. thank you. thank you & hello.

about the author

Sabrina Benaim is a writer, performance & teaching artist, whose home base is Toronto. She was a member of the Canadian championship-winning 2014 Toronto Poetry Slam team, & in 2015, she represented Toronto at the Women Of The World Poetry Slam. Sabrina has written poems for ESPNW, The Government of Canada, & most recently, made her Canadian television debut with Sport Chek, writing & voicing the third installment of their #WhatItTakes Olympic Manifesto video series. Sabrina enjoys breaking down stigma, women who help women, & the Toronto Blue Jays. She will accept any invitation to dance.